365
Things
Every
Parent
Should Know

D1636698

HARVEST HOUSE PUBLISHERS
Eugene, Oregon 97402

Scripture quoted from *The Everyday Bible, New Century Version,* copyright © 1987, 1988 by Word Publishing, Dallas, Texas 75039. Used by permission.

Published in association with the literary agency of Alive Communications, P.O. Box 49068, Colorado Springs, CO 80949.

365 THINGS EVERY PARENT SHOULD KNOW

Copyright © 1992 by Doug Fields
Published by Harvest House Publishers
Eugene, Oregon 97402

Library of Congress Cataloging-in-Publication Data

Fields, Doug, 1962-
    365 things every parent should know / Doug Fields.
      p.   cm.
    ISBN 1-56507-027-5
     1. Parenting—United States.   2. Parent and child—
United States.   3. Parenting—Religious aspects—
Christianity.   I. Title.
II. Title: Three-hundred-sixty-five things every parent
should know.
HQ755.8.F53   1992
649'.1—dc20
                                   92-13279
                                       CIP

Printed in the United States of America.

*To the parents
in the Fields and Guiso lineage, who have
handed down their personal treasures of insight
to enable their children to celebrate life.*

Introduction

There are two aspects of being a parent that are very important to me. The first is that I want to learn as much as I can from whomever I can. I read books on parenting, I rent parent-instructional videos, I clip articles, I watch other parents, I interview parents, and I even eavesdrop on conversations relating to parenting. I want to learn how to be a better parent!

The second vital aspect of parenting for me, is acquiring wisdom. Anyone can be a learner, but wisdom involves *applying* truths and being willing to grow and change. I desire to be wise with what I learn and intentional with the limited opportunities I have with my children. When I read in Proverbs to "cry out for wisdom," my prayer is that the tears of parents will bring knowledge and understanding.

We have significant responsibilities and privileges as parents. It's because of this significance that I want to pass along this small book of truths I've learned along the way and am in the midst of applying on a daily basis. Obviously this list isn't conclusive, but I trust that many of these insights will help, inspire, challenge, and motivate you as you influence one of God's greatest gifts . . . your children.

Every Parent Should Know . . .

1

which restaurants let
kids eat for free.

2

children follow heroes
but need models.

Every Parent Should Know . . .

3

**puppy love is very
real to puppies.**

4

**it's okay to get
messy.**

5

---

things are different
today than when parents
were children.

6

---

a well-stocked refrigerator
can have nothing
to eat.

7

kids love to win—
especially against parents.

8

the best way to end
a doctor's appointment
is with a milk shake.

9

children
don't know the
correct answer to
"How many times
do I have to
tell you . . ."

10

---

five action Bible
stories.

11

---

to freely dispense
Band-Aids, even when
there is no blood.

12

public kisses
become unwanted
by age ten,
but that doesn't
mean they should
be stopped.

13

at least one
silly family secret.

14

normal children hate
taking baths, brushing teeth,
and changing underwear.

15

a child needs one-on-one
attention.

16

fast food should be
a treat and not a diet.

17

an explanation for
where dead animals "go."

18

it is good for men
and boys to cry.

19

---

a night light is
comforting to young
children.

20

---

how to slay killer
monsters.

21

how to play their
child's favorite game.

22

a child's problems
may seem insignificant,
but they can be
overwhelming to a child.

23

mementoes
and souvenirs may
be overpriced and
poorly made, but
they can provide
lasting family
memories.

24

---

that changes
can be enjoyed.

25

---

their child wants to
be trusted.

26

how to be an active
listener to their child.

27

children need exercise.

Every Parent Should Know . . .

28

public discipline can be
more devastating
than constructive.

29

how to apply sunscreen.

Every Parent Should Know . . .

30

children want to hear
how their parents
fell in love.

31

children are a gift
from the Lord
(Psalm 127:3).

32

when children ask
for help with homework,
they're looking
for an answer
and not a 30-minute
lecture on the origin
of the subject.

33

not to leave children
under ten years of age
at home alone.

34

to avoid labels—
they're best on jars.

35

children forget.

36

the common cold
can't be caught from
going barefoot.

37

their child's teachers.

38

boys need a
father figure.

39

how to throw a Frisbee.

40

every child has
a talent.

41

how to make up
a convincing answer
to a question
with no answer
so the child
will stop asking.

Every Parent Should Know . . .

42

how to get rid
of "kid stains"
like grass, grape juice,
and catsup.

43

criticism is painful.

Every Parent Should Know . . .

44

the benefits of creating a
positive family motto.

45

how to encourage
responsibility.

46

the more complex
life becomes, the
more simple truths
should be applied.

47

what temperature
constitutes a fever.

Every Parent Should Know . . .

48

how to help
their children make
something special for
the parent of honor
on Mother's Day
and Father's Day.

49

to encourage creativity
and allow young minds
to imagine.

50

it is virtually impossible
for a small child to
understand divorce.

51

children need to be
given responsibilities within
the family.

52

what captures their
child's attention.

53

whether their child
is proud to bring
friends home.

54

how to identify if
their discipline was fair,
too harsh, or too lenient.

55

children feel comforted
when they see their
parents are in love.

56

how to encourage their
children to practice.

Every Parent Should Know . . .

57

children won't remember
if the cake was bought
or homemade,
but they will remember
whether or not they
had a party.

58

children can be the most
creative when they're
a little bored.

59

when to give their
children space.

60

Jesus said,
"You must accept
the kingdom of God
as a little child
accepts things, or you
will never enter it"
(Mark 10:15).

61

family vacations provide
life-long memories.

62

not every minute of a
child's life has to be
filled with classes,
tutoring, or sports.

63

---

how to explain basic
Christian truths in
language they can
understand.

64

---

how to negotiate.

65

how to spell
"lackadaisical."

66

children need to be taught
that adults can be wrong.

67

God's love is
perfect.

68

no child arrives
in this world with an
owner's manual.

69

children notice their
parents' drinking patterns.

70

celebrating the smallest
signs of progress
encourages better results.

71

a home
filled with laughter,
pranks, jokes,
and silliness
is a
happy home.

72

how to make a puppet
from an airline
disposal bag.

73

their child's attitude
will affect success
more than his skills.

Every Parent Should Know . . .

74

how to choose good books
for their children.

75

how to help their
children recognize people
in need.

76

when to apologize.

77

patience is a quality
that pays great rewards
over a lifetime.

78

a good leader
in the church is one
whose children exercise
obedience and respect
(see 1 Timothy 3:4).

79

as a teenager,
David killed Goliath
and was used by God.

80

each of their children
is an original masterpiece
created by God.

81

how to complain
about lousy television
programs.

82

how to teach their
children to resolve
conflicts.

83

academic success
during grade school
or high school
isn't always an
indicator of success
in college.

84

how to communicate
unconditional love.

85

how to laugh at their
own failures.

Every Parent Should Know . . .

86

how to
pay attention
to what is *really*
going on
within the heart
and mind of a child.

87

---

their child's favorite
dessert.

88

---

how to nurture learning
through involvement.

Every Parent Should Know . . .

89

when to bite their
tongues.

90

how to recognize
progress.

91

a child's
perception is always
true to him
regardless of
what the parent
may believe.
His perception
is fact.

92

dozens of ways to say
"I love you."

93

how to lead a child
to Christ.

94

grown children are
usually thankful for
parental discipline.

95

when to say,
"That's enough."

96

how to model
integrity.

97

the importance of
setting aside a
homework time
for children.

Every Parent Should Know . . .

98

how to help children
understand consequences
for behavior.

99

how to instill respect
in their children
by showing respect
for them.

Every Parent Should Know . . .

100

the average
American father spends
less than five
minutes a day
with his children
in education and
communication.

101

an entertaining
"war story" about
their days growing up.

102

children are experiencing
adult privileges much sooner
than their parents did.

103

their counterpart on
television usually plays
the fool while the
children appear wise
and mature.

104

encouragement is like
oxygen to the heart.

Every Parent Should Know . . .

105

Moses said, "Anyone
who says cruel things
to his father or mother
must be put to death"
(Exodus 21:17).
How is that for
a threat?

106

morals are best taught
by parents.

107

how much it means
to children when parents
attend their events.

108

the physical and emotional
transitions from childhood,
through adolescence, and
into young adulthood.

109

failure goes hand-in-hand
with growth.

110

children often perceive
pressure to be perfect
from their parents.

111

they can't protect
children from all
problems.

Every Parent Should Know . . .

112

how to build
character.

113

a few current Top Forty
song titles.

Every Parent Should Know . . .

114

to phone their children
when they are out of town.

115

the danger signs
of drug abuse.

Every Parent Should Know . . .

116

how to pray with their
children.

117

how to teach
children to search
for the right answers.

Every Parent Should Know . . .

118

the good person
who lives an
honest life
is a blessing to
his children
(Proverbs 20:7).

119

---

to teach their chidren
to ask questions.

120

---

how to save for a
child's education.

121

to value knowledge
over grades.

122

how to model spiritual
maturity.

Every Parent Should Know . . .

123

how to ask
"how-do-you-feel" questions.

124

a nearby animal
shelter.

125

there are
approximately
20,000 implied
sexual acts
on television
each year,
nearly all
of them outside
of marriage.

Every Parent Should Know . . .

126

children watch
22 to 25 hours of TV
each week.

127

how to talk openly
and honestly about
sexuality.

Every Parent Should Know . . .

128

writing
frequent notes
and letters to their
children builds a
strong foundation for
communication.

Every Parent Should Know . . .

129

how to act
silly.

130

ways to honor their
child's feelings.

Every Parent Should Know . . .

131

when to be a
good loser.

132

how to discipline
without destroying
character.

133

if a person does not
punish his children,
he does not love them.
But the person who loves
his children is careful
to correct them
(Proverbs 13:24).

134

to show love and
approval regardless
of the report card.

135

it's more important
to learn *how* to think
than *what* to think.

Every Parent Should Know . . .

136

where to find information
on current drug
trends.

137

when to replace
lecturing with calm
questioning.

138

when to point out
the positive.

139

railroad tracks
aren't safe.

140

not to withhold love
for poor performance.

141

children need thrills
to look forward to,
not possessions
to look back on.

142

to compliment every
hand-made project.

143

the theology of
grace.

144

children who have it all
will appreciate nothing.

145

it takes approximately
three weeks to form
or break a habit.

146

---

table manners will
improve.

147

---

children would rather work
at a neighbor's home.

Every Parent Should Know . . .

148

to encourage their child
in front of others.

149

when to buy their child
headphones.

150

democracy doesn't always
work in the home.

151

to find fault with
what the child has done,
not who the child is.

152

to expect the
unexpected.

153

children seek
significance like adults
seek money.

154

to take suicide threats
seriously.

155

trying to win over
a child may
eventually make
him a loser.

Every Parent Should Know . . .

156

a few of Murphy's
laws.

157

how to cool off
before reacting.

Every Parent Should Know . . .

158

when a hug is needed.

159

children love to see their
parents break the rules.

Every Parent Should Know ...

160

that it
takes more love
to say no
to the pressures
of buying
than it does to
give in.

161

one consequence of
punishment is more
effective than ten
lectures or threats.

162

a misbehaving child
is a discouraged one.

Every Parent Should Know . . .

163

to call attention to
what the child does well.

164

popularity is sought
after by kids, but
parents are rarely
ever popular.

Every Parent Should Know . . .

165

the names of the
seven dwarfs.

166

kids don't believe
their parents walked
through miles of snow
to get to school.

167

---

every child
is full of
foolishness.
But punishment
can get
rid of it
(Proverbs 22:15).

168

photographs are
priceless.

169

they must weigh
their words wisely;
a spoken word
can't be erased.

170

puberty makes kids
strange and parents weird.

171

long adult conversations
are boring.

Every Parent Should Know . . .

172

how to develop
an attitude of grace
by expecting and
allowing failure.

173

children are
expensive.

174

children are
priceless.

175

during adolescence
the phone never belongs
to the parent.

Every Parent Should Know . . .

176

at least once they
will be called "the worst
parents in the world."

177

buying at least
one Disney video
is a good investment.

178

children hate
to sit.

179

affection is a blanket
of love.

Every Parent Should Know . . .

180

to knock before entering
a child's room.

181

the best earplugs
are found at sporting
goods stores.

Every Parent Should Know . . .

182

their child
is the target of
multimillion-dollar
ad campaigns created
to establish product
loyalty.

183

a child's friend
will probably have
nicer parents.

184

how to calculate
a batting average.

Every Parent Should Know . . .

185

adolescents don't want
to be seen in public
with their parents.

186

a child's allowance
is never enough.

Every Parent Should Know . . .

187

how
to make a
butterfly bandage
to decrease bleeding
while a child waits
for stitches.

188

it's okay to use
a "do not disturb" sign
on their bedroom door.

189

a few magic tricks.

190

at least one boastful
story about their
childhood.

191

the answers to
every childhood question.

Every Parent Should Know . . .

192

rules will be broken.

193

how to respond when
rules are broken.

194

where to buy discount
clothing.

195

kids need to read
and be read to.

196

when to take a
vacation.

197

how to pack a picnic
basket.

198

the opening day of the
local baseball team.

199

how to make a
flour-and-salt dough map.

200

how to make a mansion
with sugar cubes.

201

how to pack a
lunch bag that will
be the envy of others.

202

young children
want their parents
to go on at least
one field trip
with their class.

Every Parent Should Know . . .

203

potty training should
not be pushed unless the
child is an adolescent.

204

how to teach their
children to ask
questions.

205

CPR and the Heimlich maneuver.

206

every birthday needs a special celebration and memory.

207

to save report cards,
art projects, and
favorite originals.

208

house pets can teach
responsibility.

Every Parent Should Know . . .

209

how to give freedom while
maintaining respect.

210

Correct your child and
you will be proud of him.
He will give you pleasure
(Proverbs 29:17).

211

to keep an emergency
gift hidden for a
spontaneous celebration.

212

a traditional family
recipe to pass on.

213

the tooth fairy exists
up to age eight—
beyond that,
the kids are faking it
for the cash.

214

a well-stocked purse
includes gum, candy,
a pencil, paper, and
tissue.

215

how to find double
coupons.

216

Sunday school teachers
should always be
thanked.

217

what local summer
programs are being
offered.

218

drive-in movies can
be a great family
tradition.

219

to keep the treat
jar full.

Every Parent Should Know . . .

220

how to involve children
in family decisions.

221

fingerprint their
child.

Every Parent Should Know . . .

222

to have emergency
phone numbers handy.

223

to give their child
a piggy bank.

Every Parent Should Know . . .

224

what expectations
to keep low.

225

God understands the
pain of a suffering
child.

Every Parent Should Know . . .

226

to share about
their day.

227

how to scare
the monsters out from
underneath the bed.

Every Parent Should Know . . .

228

how to encourage
participation.

229

the importance of
frequent family
activities.

Every Parent Should Know . . .

230

not to make their
children angry but
raise them with the
training and teaching
of the Lord
(see Ephesians 6:4).

Every Parent Should Know . . .

231

how to reward
their children.

232

a little humor
goes a long way.

Every Parent Should Know . . .

233

how to talk openly
about drugs and alcohol.

234

Babe Ruth struck out
more often than he
hit home runs . . .
and so will parents.

235

children are not
miniature adults.

236

the best is all
they can do.

Every Parent Should Know . . .

237

someone to turn to
for help during a
time of need.

238

the location of the
nearest emergency room.

239

the importance of
laughter.

240

to work harder
at finding the good
in children than in
pointing out the bad.

241

to display a child's
original artwork
around the house.

242

television quenches
creativity while reading
nurtures it.

Every Parent Should Know . . .

243

the location of a
children's museum.

244

the story-hour at a
local library.

Every Parent Should Know . . .

245

discipline and punishment
are not the same.

246

seat belts save
lives.

247

five free activities
families can enjoy
together.

248

the date of their
church's next weekend
marriage renewal.

Every Parent Should Know . . .

249

how to encourage
their child's decision-
making skills.

250

a recipe for French
toast.

251

---

not to nag
their children.
If parents are
too hard to please,
children may want to
stop trying
(Colossians 3:21).

252

a good relaxation
technique—prayer.

253

not to share comparisons
with their children.

254

a few bedtime antics
to help children fall
asleep.

255

home should be an
emotionally safe
place.

Every Parent Should Know...

256

complex
carbohydrates,
like pasta and
breads, are the
most efficient source
of energy to help
children get through
the day.

257

how to help their child
identify put-downs
and compliments.

258

how to create a
"Picasso-piece-of-art"
from scraps around
the house.

Every Parent Should Know . . .

259

how to throw a
birthday party.

260

what motivates their
child.

Every Parent Should Know . . .

261

the importance of
taking time for their
marriage.

262

how to teach tolerance
by example.

Every Parent Should Know . . .

263

how they're going to
respond if and when a
child quits a commitment.

264

quality time and
quantity time are
both vital.

265

love is a verb.

266

how to accept
less-than-perfect results.

Every Parent Should Know . . .

267

when to put the
television in the closet.

268

how to encourage
sportsmanship.

Every Parent Should Know . . .

269

there is always a
more difficult way to
do something.

270

how to maximize
summertime.

Every Parent Should Know . . .

271

children
don't always believe,
understand, or
follow the
principles that parents
are most passionate
about.

272

to help children
take responsibility
for their actions.

273

"not me" actually means
"I'm scared, I blew it,
but I don't want to
admit it."

274

their own blind spots.

275

not to major on the
minors.

276

the best gift they can
give their child is a
happy marriage.

277

few parents, on their
deathbed, wish they had
spent more time working.

Every Parent Should Know ...

278

how to use the
encyclopedia.

279

something about their
child they can
brag about.

280

to excel in one
area of parenting—
have a specialty.

281

a child's reasoning
isn't always rational.

282

their children
know when they are
fighting with each other.

283

that children are
smarter than they
appear.

Every Parent Should Know . . .

284

children hear everything
they say.

285

grudges don't persuade.

Every Parent Should Know . . .

286

the phrase
"Do as I say and
not as I do"
has little credibility
with children.

287

income is disposable
but children are not.

288

the map of the world.

Every Parent Should Know . . .

289

how to recognize
a good school.

290

the family that
prays together stays
together.

Every Parent Should Know . . .

291

how to contribute to
a child's classroom.

292

children use their
parents' attitude toward
them to validate
their identity.

Every Parent Should Know . . .

293

how to convert a
weakness into a
strength.

294

when to make their
children "pay the
freight."

Every Parent Should Know . . .

295

how to record
and preserve positive
memories.

296

to be generous with
encouragement.

Every Parent Should Know . . .

297

how to establish
realistic expectations
for their children.

298

how to establish
and communicate
boundaries.

299

punishment and
correction make a
child wise.
If he is left to do
as he pleases, he will
disgrace his mother
(Proverbs 29:15).

Every Parent Should Know...

300

television is a
constant source of
negative values.

301

how to comfort a
heartbroken child.

Every Parent Should Know . . .

302

a child with godly parents
will never be poor.

303

how to inspire their
children to make a
difference in this world.

Every Parent Should Know . . .

304

adolescence
means love notes,
chasing the
opposite sex, and
falling in and out
of love at least
once a day.

Every Parent Should Know . . .

305

how to express
affection.

306

at least five
entertaining activities
to replace television.

307

the importance of
eating meals together.

308

the parents of their
child's friends.

Every Parent Should Know . . .

309

the words to
"Cat's in the Cradle."

310

children learn by
watching their parents.

Every Parent Should Know . . .

311

a "cheer-up" recipe for
a difficult moment.

312

material gifts will soon
become boring if a child
has no happiness
in his heart.

313

half of American
adolescents are sexually
active.

314

good memories should
far outnumber the
bad ones.

Every Woman Should Know...

315

how to discuss the
lyrics of their children's
music without attacking.

316

successful education
begins in the home.

317

they will feel like
maids if children don't
have chores.

318

what's "hot" for Nintendo
isn't necessarily best
for their child.

Every Parent Should Know . . .

319

if they "shop till
they drop," their children
will "cry if they can't buy."

320

avoiding retaliation
requires maturity
but produces security.

Every Parent Should Know . . .

321

to go on "dates"
with their child.

322

the name of the
school nurse.

323

---

raising
a child with
character
is more impressive
than raising
one with a
trophy case full
of awards.

324

character is built
through discovery and
failure.

325

a kind word
won't be forgotten.

326

"runaways" often
return by dusk.

327

a few good travel
games for the car.

Every Parent Should Know ...

328

communication
improves when you
eat meals
with the phone
off the hook
and the television
turned off.

Every Parent Should Know ...

329

to become punctual ...
sooner or later.

330

the titles of the
top five children's videos.

Every Parent Should Know . . .

331

at least one restaurant
that "appreciates" small
children.

332

to cover the
refrigerator with
"masterpieces."

333

---

to write their children's
initials on clothes
before sending the
kids away to camp.

334

---

small hands don't work
the same as big ones.

335

even
a child is known
by his behavior.
His actions show
if he is
innocent and good
(Proverbs 20:11).

336

a child's appetite
will vary from day to day.

337

a gun left around
the house will probably
be played with.

Every Parent Should Know . . .

338

how to diffuse jealousy
among siblings.

339

overcontrolling stifles
the development of healthy
decision-making skills.

Every Parent Should Know . . .

340

car rides
provide a
quality opportunity
for conversations
and bonding—
if parents will
take it.

Every Parent Should Know . . .

341

to praise their
child daily.

342

intimidation doesn't
produce long-term results.

343

the more toys they
give to counteract
boredom, the more the
kids will demand.

344

how to whisper.

345

unconditional love
is a risk.

346

they can do the best
job they are capable
of doing and let God
help with the rest.

347

to play board games
with children on
rainy days.

348

a child's behavior
often reflects their
home situation.

349

their child better than
anyone alive.

350

they don't have to be
rocket scientists to
be great parents.

351

they don't have to
fulfill their child's
wish-list.

352

high-priced shoes
won't make their child
a better athlete.

353

decisions about a
child's discipline will
rarely be democratic.

354

children will fall off
swings and make
lousy decisions.

355

not to complain
about their child's loud
music if they gave him
the stereo for Christmas.

356

the exceptions to
the rules.

357

discipline has consequences
as well as hugs, kisses,
and tears.

358

there are no perfect
parents.

359

how to avoid the
candy aisle while
shopping.

360

if their family sleeps
during church, it may be
time to switch churches.

Every Parent Should Know . . .

361

spit-up can be
washed out.

362

there won't be teenage
attitudes in heaven.

Every Parent Should Know . . .

363

how to bake cookies
with their child.

364

a happy family is an
earlier heaven.

Every Parent Should Know . . .

365

Jesus said, "Let the
little children come to me. . . .
The kingdom of heaven
belongs to people who are
like these children"
(Matthew 19:14).

About the Author

Doug Fields, founder and director of *Making Young Lives Count* is a national public speaker, college professor, and author of over 12 books including *Creative Romance*, and *Too Old, Too Soon*. He served for over ten years as senior youth pastor at South Coast Community Church.

For further information regarding *Making Young Lives Count*, write Doug Fields at:

Making Young Lives Count
4330 Barranca Parkway
Suite 101-346
Irvine, CA 92715.